SWAN

SONG

WINNER OF THE 2020 FROST PLACE
CHAPBOOK COMPETITION

SWAN SONG

poems

ARMEN DAVOUDIAN

BULL★CITY
PRESS

DURHAM, NORTH CAROLINA

Swan Song

Winner of the 2020 Frost Place Chapbook Competition
Selected by Patrick Donnelly

Library of Congress Cataloging-in-Publication Data
Davoudian, Armen
Swan Song: poems / by Armen Davoudian
p. cm.
ISBN-13: 978-1-949344-17-2

Published in the United States of America

Cover painting by Arshile Gorky
Cover design by Savannah Bradley
Book design by Spock and Associates
Author photo by Matthew Lansburgh

Published by
BULL CITY PRESS
1217 Odyssey Drive
Durham, NC 27713
www.BullCityPress.com

CONTENTS

BLACK GARLIC

All over Sofeh Mountain, sensing life,
garlic escapes its winter sleep in scapes
we cut and bind together in a sheaf,
the skinned cloves sticky to the touch like lips,
firm but fleshy, reeking as though alive.
We weave a garland to hang round the clock
and can the rest. Grandma says she'll save
the biggest jar to open when I'm back.

I found a strand of silver hair today
snagged on the label of a jar, a gray
entangled cursive of another language.
Inside, the broken heads soften and age
in verjuice, coriander, salt, molasses,
black with sulfuration, new with loss.

COMING OUT OF THE SHOWER

I shut my eyes under the scalding stream,
      scrubbing off last night's dream,
when suddenly I hear your voice again
    as though it caught in the clogged drain

and was sent bubbling back up from the other
      world where you're not my mother.
This time it's really you. I'm really here.
    I blink. We do not disappear.

Dad left, you say, to shower at the shop
      so I don't need to stop
just yet—and yet I do, unable to
    resume old customs, unlike you.

In a one-bath four-person household, we
      learned what we mustn't see,
become, in time, so coolly intimate
    with one another's silhouette

behind the opaque frosted shower screen
      that once more stands between
us two. While at the mirror you apply
    foundation and concealer, I

wash out my hair with argan oil shampoo,
        which means I'll smell like you
all day. *Mama*, I shout, *I'm coming out*,
        and as you look away I knot

around me tight your lavender robe de chambre,
        cinching my waist, and clamber
out of the tub, taking care not to step
        outside the cotton mat and drip

on the cracked floor you've polished with such zeal
        we're mirrored in each tile.
Yet, you'd forgive the spillage, or forget.
        What else will you love me despite?

TRANSITION LENSES

I am young.

Everyone in my all-boys school is dumber than me.

It is an Armenian Christian school,

it is a Muslim country.

Our classroom has big windows.

On sunny days, no one can tell

where I am looking. I read *The Count of Monte Cristo*

inside my physics textbook. I draw pictures of naked women

for my classmates, who fold them into planes

and fly them across the room. There is a long staircase

down the hall. On exam day,

my friends sit on the steps with their shirts unbuttoned.

I write the answers on their chests in my absurdly small hand.

SAFFRON RICE

Piled like a treasure-hoard and studded gold,
mounds and mounds of it, and the women hunched

in dark, silent bundles in corners here and there,
somebody's live-in grandmother or widowed aunt

muttering inaudibly and huddled on the ground,
as we ran from room to room before dinner

in a stranger's house with strange smells,
patchouli funk in the spare room, patchwork blankets

and stale old rugs stacked high to form guest beds,
the coy eligible girls rinsed in so much rosewater

it would coat your tongue, the mulish reek
of stiff-necked single young men gangling

over the tittering crowd for O a glimpse
of that one's ankle, O a snatch of that one's hairline,

the never-ending circus buzzing on
until relief washes the room and always

you're called back to the perfectly bland perfume
you crave in sickness, your face grown sallow,

of just rice, mounds and mounds of it, tinted yellow.

THE YELLOW SWAN

I love the black swan.
>   —James Merrill, "The Black Swan"

At noon the pedaled swans afloat midstream
              or parked at the water's rim
find the boy first in line or there before
there is a line, and always the nice boatman
lets him mount his favorite ride, whose name
              defies all rust and wear.
       He whispers, *I love the yellow swan,*

a secret he knows better than to share
              save in the hollow ear-
like curve of that arched neck whose mirror image
breaks on rings of water as he climbs
between the wings and pedals from the pier,
              a trail of molted plumage
       shuddering in his wake. The river foams,

churned by the paddlewheel and changed to ocean,
              its surface cut by the question
mark of the swan—no, dragon—gliding on
the hissing bloodstained waters as he turns
fire on darkness, almost wins his mission
              while his parents chat in the sun,
       unaware of all that burns

down on the other bank. But like most love
      the swan-ride is cut off.
The stroke of one o'clock returns the beast
to boat, the boat to boatman. He hates the boatman.
He hates his parents, whom he won't forgive.
      He hates the girl who's next.
    Poor boy, he hates the yellow swan.

PASSAGE

A boy shoulders his way
through the thighs of men
(musk of fenugreek)
and shucks off his book bag.
Because he is a boy,
he rides the sluggish bus
with purpose, knuckles tight
around the tall steel stanchion.
Out the window, a patch
of magenta screeches by,
tulips loud as the color
of dyed chicks.

                  Far west,
they are wrapping children in Mylar
and putting them to sleep
where they used to house ammo.
A mother shouts, *te amo*.

27 MARJAN STREET

The rooms shrink down with each new coat of paint.
The house stays calm. The child inside the house
is also calm, face tucked into mother's blouse,
but the rooms shrink down with each new coat of paint.

Though the house is gone, the walls will not relent.
No more a child, at every new impasse,
you shrink the rooms with coat on coat of paint
to a house inside that child inside that house.

ARARAT

When I left home I thought I was the raven
sounding the future for echoes of my voice.
Sunlight tore and stitched back sea and heaven,
and daily I renewed my prodigal choice.
Never, never. I turned my own name over
above the raving ocean, content to watch
my shadow and my image almost touch
once every day, forever and forever.

But when did I swap feathers with the dove,
coughing up splinters from the olive branch
I'll never carry back? The shattered conch
of Noah's ark was dug up from its grave,
but this is where I live now. Should I cry?
Coo. Caw. My house is made of straw.

مرگ قو

مهدی حمیدی شیرازی

شنیدم که چون قوی زیبا بمیرد

فریبنده زاد و فریبا بمیرد

شب مرگ تنها نشیند به موجی

رود گوشه‌ای دور و تنها بمیرد

در آن گوشه چندان غزل خواند آن شب

که خود در میان غزل‌ها بمیرد

گروهی بر آنند کاین مرغ شیدا

کجا عاشقی کرد، آنجا بمیرد

شب مرگ از بیم آنجا شتابد

که از مرگ غافل شود تا بمیرد

من این نکته گیرم که باور نکردم

ندیدم که قویی به صحرا بمیرد

چو روزی ز آغوش دریا برآمد

شبی هم در آغوش دریا بمیرد

تو دریای من بودی آغوش واکن

که می‌خواهد این قوی زیبا بمیرد

SWAN SONG

after Mehdi Hamidi Shirazi

They say when the time comes for a swan to die,
it goes where other swans have gone to die.

They say as the last night begins to fall,
it trails behind the setting sun to die.

And it sings ghazals, as though it wished between
the pages of its own diwan to die.

They say a swan loves only once and will
return to where its love was won to die.

Making its deathbed where it first made love,
it can forget it has withdrawn to die.

Are these tales true? In the desert, where I live,
no swan has come, not a single one, to die.

But then they say that swans return to water,
in whose embrace life was begun, to die.

Open your arms, my dear, and slake my thirst:
the time has come for one more swan to die.

HARPER'S FERRY

And then we came to the famous confluence
of two great rivers, the Shenandoah gray

and cloudy, the Potomac blue and clear.
A footbridge, weighted with lovers' padlocks, hung

to our left. The propped-up beak of Jefferson Rock
rose above the spruces to our right.

You wore your jacket tied around your waist.
Bluebells nodded at our feet. We heard

the clownish yak of nuthatches and saw
the reddest tulips I'd ever seen, each cup

open and pitch-black at the core, as though
a cigarette had been put out in it.

SOMETHING THERE IS
THAT DOESN'T LOVE

We're in Deutsche camp,
which is a tasteless joke
my friend with the undercut
trolls out of history
like a limp goldfish pulled
out of its bowl. In fact
we're in Middlebury, VT,
summer of '14,
and I've vowed to unlearn English
for six weeks, so I can get
more Rilke and an A.

But mostly we play soccer,
shirtless against the shirts,
and afterward we screw
as twenty-somethings do.
We even fall in love,
whispering in the dark
of the campus graveyard
under the sacred oath
of German 101:
—*Ich liebe dich, mein Liebling!*
—*Und ich dich liebe auch!*

Weekends we go to Ripton
to hike the Robert Frost
Interpretive Trail.
Yes, there's a wood with a road
splitting in it, a pile
of timber forever rotting
with the *burning of decay*
(for *the world will end in fire*)
and last, the wall! Its faded
placard reads, *Something
there is that doesn't love.*

It's 2016,
all that is history.
Now I know *lieben* from *leben*,
but Rilke in German feels
like a fish out of water.
The president believes
good fences make good neighbors.
The roads remain divided.
Undercuts are in.
Something that doesn't love
burns on the streets again.

TRAVEL BAN

Warned of copperheads and rattlesnakes,
I poke a stick into the underbrush
before each coddled step. Behind, my friend,
shins itching still with pain, hobbles in fear
of every three-pronged leaf. Cautious invaders
of the grass, we wade the muddy floodplain veined
with rivulets of thirst. Slowly, finally,
we reach the stingy bramble of blackberry
and drown our lips into the sour blood.
A fuzz of rain has ripened on the air,
enough to dull the early stars and toads
now coming on and going off, enough
to snag on skin like sap from wounded wood.
And in my ears are the words your father said
last October, phoned in from Kabul
for your wedding, the Dari sounding itchingly
off to my ear like a favorite childhood stew
made by someone else's mother and eaten
in someone else's house, and stranger still
in the Afghan interpreter's muddled English: *My lips
are singing on your wedding day, my son,
but my heart in me is crying.* The walls of this house
are crying and all the things of the world are crying,
the sky and the night are crying and the owls and the toads,
and the wood toad toy you gave me before your wedding
from a local art festival in Roswell, Georgia,
with the dowel in its mouth that's used to ring

a rigid croaking off the beveled lips
ribbed on its spine. I roll the pen-sized dowel
down each wooden vertebra and pass
to your spine, bony like a fisted knuckle,
and then your father's, one by one wearing on
the bone-knots of the old man in Kabul.
The rain is falling harder. Separately,
each touching his own body, we wash off
any lingering trace of poison ivy.

RUBAIYAT

I shake sand from the pages of my book.
As you change out of your trunks, I try to look
   away. Last night the sheets were stiff, crinkly
as paper, sand inside each crease and nook.

  ::::

We strip and plunge into the phosphorescence
of blooming plankton. Your naked body glistens
   in the bitter brine we will pass back and forth
between our lips tonight as friendship lessens.

  ::::

Another day we're locked inside as rain
needles the surface of the sea again.
   You dunk a graham cracker in your tea
too long, then pour the thin sludge down the drain.

  ::::

It was too late. You slapped a mosquito dead
on my neck. Nights afterward, turning in bed,
   the sheets are rough. I try to fight the urge
to scratch. I shut my eyes. You're in my head.

ALIBI

We sat together in the country
where men like us can sit together
like this. It was night, your blond hair full
of moonlight. You took
one socked foot out of a loafer
and held it in your hand.
How easy, then, to have said, *I love you.*
We drank from the same bottle.
How easy to have meant it too.

Later, in the obvious light
of the train you are almost too late for, I can see again
why we settled
for what was difficult.

PERSIAN POETRY

I teach Robert Lowell to undergraduates at an elite institution.
My colleagues study poverty, whiteness,
the impossibility
of language to signify, and the moral imperative of art.
You pinch your thumb and index finger
into the obscene gesture for peace
while the endowed lecture on the figure of the otter in modern British poetry
continues. Your face is suitably hairy
and preoccupied, your hand
placed absurdly high on your thigh.
The words are dull and fashionable, positionality,
Englishness, paradigm shift, *other*-ness—
the wordplay cheap and without tact.
You are taking dutiful notes on your electronic notebook.
Ambiguity, imperial construct, republican feminism.
Your knuckles are furred like my father's,
balling his socks one inside the other
and tossing them on the bed
for my mother to collect later.
I believe in nothing more than in love.
Yet I study English poetry
because Persian would have been too obvious.

CHIMES FOR JM

in all that pain an element of play
  —James Merrill, "Chimes for Yahya"

"Lit by far-off daylight, Isfahan,"
spirited like shahtush through the ring
of your delicious "Chimes," lights on my tongue
thirst for that old "peculiar" taste: ghalyán
smoke bittersweet like sugared tea. Unspun
discarded "cardings" (another sheepish pun
brushed under) fade to unveil that sunlit town
where my childhood river used to run.

Where's my childhood river? Used up and run
dry, its water dammed and rationed now.
Back then, JM, you would have seen it flow
with pattern rich as the yarns Yahya spun
over your eyes, trompe-l'eau of mirrored swan
catamarans twice doubled and made one.

SWAN BOATS

Mute like the reflections they have lost
or like the real birds they themselves reflect,
a flock of boats brood over the mud-cracked
script of the riverbed. No pentecost
decodes the silent babel of this tongue
whose ramifying kufic chokes the land.
The faceless surface breaks in surfs of sand.
Time out of mind, this was our turquoise blue

mind out of time, watching white thoughts come, go
across a mirror which, unchanged by them,
itself was change and could reverse the down-
ward wish of light, the headlong wash of stone
skipped on its current. Nothing is the same.
When the swans break, it won't be into song.

ACKNOWLEDGMENTS

My thanks to the following publications, where these poems first appeared, sometimes in different versions:

Bat City Review: "27 Marjan Street," "Chimes for JM"

The Greensboro Review: "Travel Ban"

The Hopkins Review: "Rubaiyat," "Swan Boats"

Literary Matters: "Coming Out of the Shower," "Swan Song," "The Yellow Swan"

The Margins: "Persian Poetry"

The Michigan Quarterly Review: "Saffron Rice"

Narrative Magazine: "Harper's Ferry"

The Offing: "Alibi"

Shenandoah: "Passage," "Something There Is That Doesn't Love"

Slate Roof Press: "Ararat"

The Southeast Review: "Black Garlic" (as "Pickled Garlic")

Thanks to Bull City Press, The Frost Place, the Lighthouse Works at Fishers' Island, and the Writing Seminars at Johns Hopkins University.

And thanks to all the teachers, editors, and friends who have supported me and my writing throughout the years. I owe a particular debt of gratitude to Christopher Childers, Patrick Donnelly, Richie Hofmann, Nick Jenkins, Dora Malech, Mary Jo Salter, John Shoptaw Alicia Stallings, Noah Stetzer, Paul Tran, and Ryan Wilson.

ABOUT THE AUTHOR

Armen Davoudian's poems and translations from Persian appear in *AGNI*, *Narrative*, *The Sewanee Review*, and elsewhere. He grew up in Isfahan, Iran, and is currently a Ph.D. candidate in English at Stanford University.

ABOUT THE FROST PLACE CHAPBOOK COMPETITION

The Frost Place is a nonprofit educational center for poetry and the arts based at Robert Frost's old homestead, which is owned by the Town of Franconia, New Hampshire. In 1976, a group of Franconia residents, led by David Schaffer and Evangeline Machlin, persuaded the Franconia town meeting to approve the purchase of the farmhouse where Robert Frost and his family lived full time from 1915 to 1920 and spent nineteen summers. A board of trustees was given responsibility for management of the house and its associated programs, which now include several conferences and seminars, readings, a museum located in the Frost farmhouse, and yearly fellowships for emerging American poets.

The Frost Place Chapbook Competition awards an annual prize to a chapbook of poems. In addition to publication of the collection by Bull City Press, the winning author receives a fellowship to The Frost Place Poetry Seminar, a cash prize, and week-long residency to live and write in The Frost Place farmhouse.

2020   Armen Davoudian, *Swan Song*
        SELECTED BY PATRICK DONNELLY

2019   Cassandra J. Bruner, *The Wishbone Dress*
        SELECTED BY EDUARDO C. CORRAL

2018   Yuki Tanaka, *Séance in Daylight*
        SELECTED BY SANDRA LIM

2017   Conor Bracken, *Henry Kissinger, Mon Amour*
        SELECTED BY DIANE SEUSS

2016   Tiana Clark, *Equilibrium*
SELECTED BY AFAA MICHAEL WEAVER

2015   Anders Carlson-Wee, *Dynamite*
SELECTED BY JENNIFER GROTZ

2014   Lisa Gluskin Stonestreet, *The Greenhouse*
SELECTED BY DAVID BAKER

2013   Jill Osier, *Should Our Undoing Come Down Upon Us White*
SELECTED BY PATRICK DONNELLY